Sculpture

Sculpture *The Shapes of Belief*

by Penelope Naylor

illustrated with photographs

◄—A FIRST BOOK—►

Franklin Watts, Inc.
845 Third Avenue
New York, N.Y. 10022

Author's note:
Due to space limitations, the beautiful sculptures
of India and the Orient, as well as the work of many
great sculptors, could not be included in this book.

Frontispiece: Michelangelo: *Pietà,* c. 1548–55, cathedral, Florence. (Scala
New York/Florence)

SBN 531-00752-9
Copyright © 1971 by Franklin Watts, Inc.
Library of Congress Catalog Card Number: 76-161070
Printed in the United States of America

Contents

Introduction

People make sculptures to give shape to the things they believe. In stone and clay, in great monuments and tiny figures, they record what they feel about life.

We can look back in time to the sculptures of distant places and see an Egyptian queen or the mask of an African chief. We can see important battles or the ordinary events of a day, the clothes and ornaments that people wore, or the games they played. We can see demons, monsters, ancestors, and idols or images of heroes and gods. We can look at the sculptures of our own age and see how the artist views his world.

But before we begin the story of sculpture we should understand what sculptures are and how they are made.

Sculpture

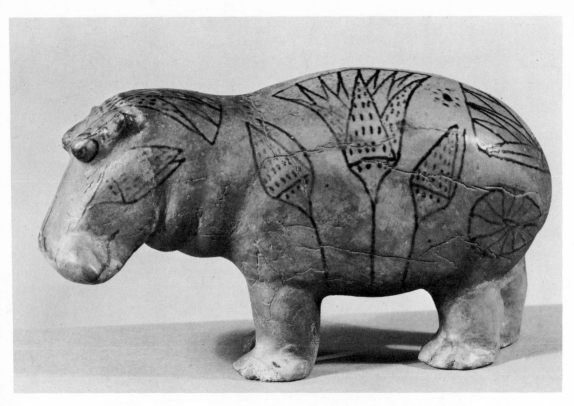

Hippopotamus, from the Tomb of Senbi, at Meir; Egyptian, XII Dynasty.
(The Metropolitan Museum of Art, Gift of Edward S. Harkness, 1917)

1/ What Is Sculpture?

Imagine that there is a little statue of a hippopotamus beside you on a table and a painting of a hippopotamus hanging on the wall. If you look at the painting, you can see it from top to bottom and from left to right. You can even touch its painted surface. But if you put your hand on the part that looks like a hippopotamus, you are really only touching a flat bit of paint. Its shape is just an illusion.

Now think of the statue. If you put your hands on it, you can feel its roundness. You can walk around it to see it from every side, and if it isn't too heavy, you can even pick it up. It has *volume*; it exists in space the way a real hippopotamus does.

The statue of the hippopotamus is sculpture. Sculpture is the art of expressing ideas through actual shape.

When the shape of a sculpture is complete from every side, like the hippopotamus, it is called *in the round,* or *freestanding* sculpture. When the shape is modeled out from a flat surface or cut into a flat surface, it is called *in relief*. Sculptures in relief do not stand

Michelangelo:
The Captive (II),
Accademia, Florence,
c. 1519. (Courtesy
of the Italian Cultural
Institute, New York)

Grave relief: Girl with Pigeons, Greek, fifth century B.C.
(The Metropolitan Museum of Art, Fletcher Fund, 1927)

by themselves, but depend on the flat surface for support, and only parts of the forms are visible.

There are two basic methods of making sculptures, whether they are freestanding or in relief: the *cutting away* and the *building up* of material. "To cut" from stone, wood, or any other hard material means that you carve away from a solid block to expose the shape you imagine to be inside. You break down one volume to create another. "To build up" material means that you construct a form from something that has no permanent shape of its own, as when you model clay or cast liquid metal. In the first case, you take material away. In the second case, you put material together. The word "sculpture" comes from the Latin word *sculpere,* which means to cut from stone, although our understanding has grown to include these other methods as well.

Each material used in sculpture has its own qualities that determine the way it can be used. Hard substances like stone, wood, and ivory are usually carved with metal tools. Softer materials like clay and plaster are modeled into shape, sometimes around an inside frame of wood or wire which is used for support. Most metals can be melted, then poured into molds which are broken away when the metal hardens, or the sculpture can be glued or welded together in pieces. These are the most commonly used materials, but there are many others, including the horns and teeth of large animals and even modern materials like plastic. The ways they have been used are as imaginative and varied as the history of sculpture itself.

2/ The Living Double

In that ancient past when man's recorded history on earth was just beginning, the idea of sculpture was born. The first sculptors were the cave dwellers of the prehistoric Stone Age, who hunted bison and other animals for food and lived in constant fear of the bears and mammoths that threatened them. Their only tools were crude pieces of stone and chipped bones, and their languages were just being formed. Their sculptures were also very crude, often just accidental scratches on the damp walls of their caves or hand prints in the wet clay of the caves' ceilings. These are not really sculptures, but they are the earliest signs of art found to date.

It took hundreds of thousands of years for these first accidental marks to develop into lines and shapes that were not accidental at all. In a period of time that lasted much longer than all of recorded history, Stone Age man gradually began to see that the marks he had made were expressions of himself and his world. He began to scratch deliberate lines on the cave walls and to make definite

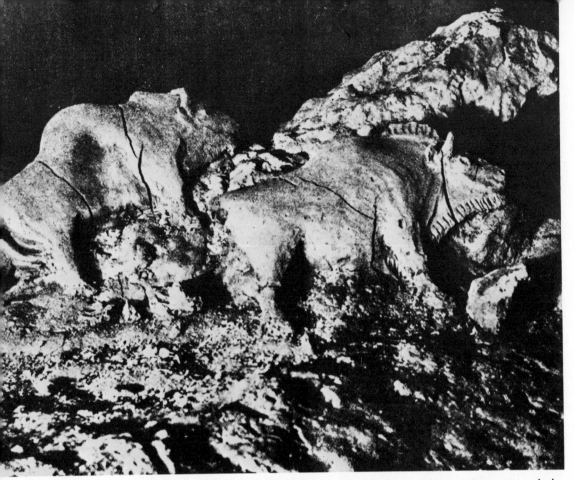

Prehistoric bisons, cave of Tuc D'Audoubert, France. (Courtesy of the American Musuem of Natural History)

patterns with his hand prints. He molded clay and mud into various shapes, just as children do with sand on the beach. Finally between 20,000 and 10,000 years ago, he was able to create the forms of animals in a naturalistic way. The animals he made represented the most powerful forces in his world, the ones directly connected to his survival: the bison and reindeer whose meat he ate and whose skins he used for clothing; the bears and mammoths that threatened his existence. He painted their images on the walls of his caves and sculptured them in bone, clay, and stone. These animals were the first true sculptures in history.

It was a magical experience to the caveman to make an image of these animals. He believed that he really *created,* that the animals he sculpted had life. They were not imitations or copies, but living doubles possessing the energy and abilities of the animals them-

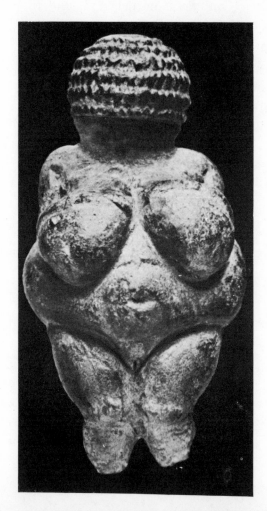

Venus of Willendorf,
Kunsthistorisches Museum, Vienna.
(The Bettmann Archive)

selves. By creating them anew, he believed that he had given himself supernatural power over their destiny. He had captured their spirits; therefore he would be able to capture them in the hunt.

The caveman also made sculptures of the human figure, but in a less realistic way. His human images were vague, like undefined shadows, their faces and personalities lost in the exaggeration of their forms. One such sculpture is the *Venus of Willendorf* (shown on page 9), named for the cave in Austria where it was found. It was carved from limestone, showing the figure of a woman with the features of her body extended as if she was soon to give birth. The caveman believed it was a symbol of motherhood, and that it would bring fertility to his clan.

Belief in the power of sculpture did not die out with the caveman. It developed as man developed, from hunting for food and living in caves to growing crops and building villages. As this change took place, man's ideas about the forces of the world also changed, and with them the magic and meaning of sculpture.

3 / Images of Magic

After following herds from season to season for more time than we can possibly recount, people finally realized that they could lead more secure lives by banding together in permanent settlements. Their tools had improved and they had discovered how to grow crops and raise animals, which provided a more reliable source of food than hunting had ever allowed. They tilled the land, sowed seeds, and reaped their harvests. They worked together with other members of their tribe and learned to honor their ancestors and their chiefs.

The forces of their world changed entirely. No longer were they dependent on the animals they hunted. They were dependent on the forces of nature, on adequate sun and rain, on the health of the land and their tribe. They dreaded the destructive forces—the storms that ruined their crops and the droughts that scorched their fields. They dreaded grass fires, disease, and famine. They gave names to these forces, both good and evil, and made ceremonies to praise or appease them. They called them *gods* and sculpted their images to give shape to what they imagined.

The images they sculpted were not true to nature as the animals of the cavemen had been. They were *exaggerations* of nature, invented to describe the superhuman qualities of the gods. The forms of people, animals, birds, and plants were combined or extended into shapes of fantasy to make new shapes that had never been seen before. In the eyes of their creators, these sculptures were signs from the supernatural world filled with magical powers.

Sculptures like these have been made all over the world from the end of the Stone Age until the present day, by people living simple tribal lives dependent on the forces of nature. Their styles may differ, but they are all expressions of supernatural beliefs made visible in similar ways. We can look at them now and understand them as a group, no matter what moment in history or point of the globe they come from.

New Guinea

Deep in the southern Pacific Ocean on the island of New Guinea live the Asmat people, who still cling to the traditions of their most ancient forebears. They believe that life began when the Great Woodcarver, Fumeripits, sculptured figures of men and women and placed them inside a sacred dwelling called the *yeu* house.

Ancestor poles, Asmat tribe, New Guinea.
(Courtesy of the Museum of Primitive Art, New York)

Fumeripits was pleased with his sculpted people, until suddenly he realized that they were only rigid statues. So he made a drum out of wood and a lizard's skin and pounded the rhythm of life for them to hear. Slowly the statues rose to their feet and started to dance, swaying their knees to the beat of the drum and moving with tiny steps, until finally they came alive. That is how man was created, say the Asmat, and since that time, they have called themselves the People of the Tree, in remembrance of the wood they were originally carved from.

Every year the Asmat reenact the myth of their creation. They go to the forest and choose fully grown mangrove trees, which they pretend to kill in a magic ceremony as if they were slaying enemies. They cut down the trees with stone axes and strip off the bark until the sap runs red. Then they carry the trees to the village, where the women greet them with victorious shouts.

In the yeu house, the sculptors wait for the trees, ready to carve images of ancestors killed in headhunting raids. Each sculptor has a style of his own, although he follows the old traditions. He cuts away large sections of wood with a stone ax, then uses shells, fish teeth, and boars' tusks to carve the smaller designs. He is limited by the shape of the tree, so he sculpts the figures one on top of the other, each standing on the head of the one beneath. When he is finished carving, he paints the figures white and the hair black, and he outlines some tattoo marks and bones with red.

Once the poles have been made, they serve as a pledge that the Asmat will revenge their ancestors' deaths by headhunting against enemy tribes. The warriors set off in their canoes, carrying wooden shields and spears, which are all carved in relief with headhunting symbols. If human heads are captured, they are brought back to the village and used in ceremonies before the poles, where the spirits of the ancestors are believed to dwell while waiting for revenge.

After the ceremonies, the poles are thrown into the forest to decay so that the ancestors' spirits will nourish the trees and the cycle can start again. In worshiping their ancestors, the Asmat constantly renew their beliefs as one generation dies and a new one takes its place. To them the world has no history; it is an unbroken chain of tradition that has remained the same for centuries.

North America

The American Indians of the Pacific Northwest made sculptures similar to the ancestor poles of the Asmat. From the trunks of tall cedar trees they carved totem poles, showing the magical animal origins of their tribes. Bold figures of different animals rose one above the other, each representing a different animal-spirit. The Indians thought they were related by blood to these animals and regarded them as family emblems. They even took the animals' names as their own and told legends of how the animals had helped the Supreme Creator to make the earth.

They carved images of Raven, who brought light to the Northwest, and of the mythical Thunderbird, who made thunder when he flapped his wings and lightning when he flashed his eyes. His folded wings were a symbol of peace. They carved images of Bear, Eagle, Salmon, Wolf, and Whale. They painted the images with colors and erected the poles in front of their houses to inspire respect for the spirits of the past.

The greatest period of totem-pole carving began about 1850,

after white traders had introduced steel tools to the Indians. The new tools allowed them to carve larger, more elaborate poles. But shortly after the traders, the missionaries came, hoping to convert the Indians to Christianity. The missionaries thought that the Indians worshiped the poles. They convinced the Indians, after telling terrifying tales of the hellfires that awaited pagans, to destroy all the existing poles and never to carve any more. Fortunately, some of the totem poles had already found their way into museums and private collections, so these symbols of the Indians' traditional beliefs were not completely destroyed.

Africa

In most parts of the African continent, sculptures have been made for hundreds of years as a vital part of life. African tribal societies sculpt many things — bowls, stools, musical instruments, and spears, as well as special statues made for religious rites. They carve these things in the images of gods and spirits, transforming even the most simple objects into symbols of magic, just as they believe that the ordinary events of their lives are signs from the supernatural world.

Many African sculptures are made in the form of masks, which are believed to be filled with the magical presence of spirits. When a man places a mask on top of his head or over his face, the spirit

inside is supposed to enter his body and change him into its personality. He then dances and moves about as if he were really possessed, while the other members of the tribe call on the spirit to protect them or give them advice.

The style and meaning of masks differ from tribe to tribe. In the Baga tribe of Guinea, a headdress mask with a face like a hawk represents the goddess of increase. In the Bambara tribe of Mali, a mask in the form of an antelope is worn during spring sowing to ensure that the crops will grow well. Other masks are used to scare off evil from the ripening harvest and to guard the graves of the dead, or as places for ancestors' spirits to dwell in the afterlife. Ghostlike masks are worn by young men when they return from initiation. Many of them are believed to have such magical powers that women and children will die if they chance to see them.

As soon as an old mask has worn out, a new one must be made. In some tribes, a sculptor is chosen by the chief of the masks and he is warned about certain taboos, for the wrong wood or tools might allow evil to enter the mask. He is then purified in a magic ceremony and sent to the forest alone, where he selects his wood and secretly begins to carve. When he has finished, he rubs the mask smooth with rough leaves and sand and polishes it with sacred liquids. Then he takes it back to the chief, who sprinkles it with an offering of animal's blood so that the spirit will live in its form. After the ritual, the old mask is discarded, as it no longer has magical powers.

Masks and sculptures in materials other than wood were made in Nigeria hundreds of years ago by the Yoruba and Bini tribes. The Yorubas developed a rich and powerful empire about A.D. 1000,

---

Mask, Songe tribe, Congo-Kinshasa.
(Courtesy of the Museum of Primitive Art, New York)

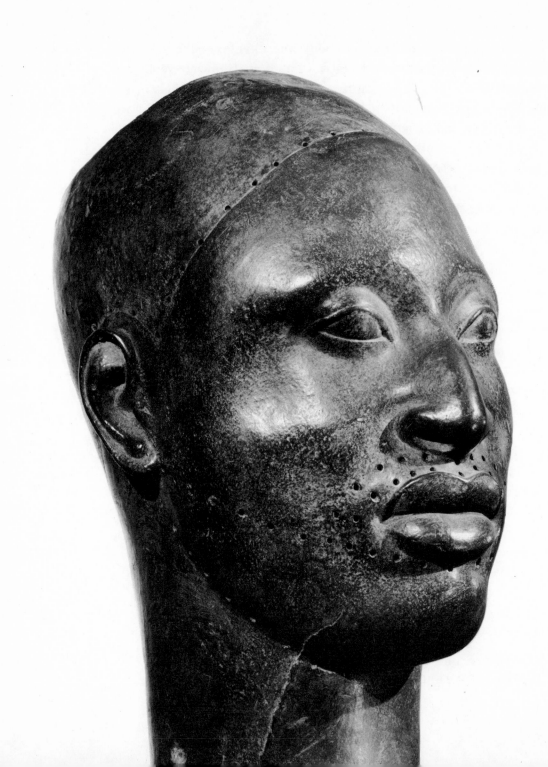

with their capital at Ife. They discovered how to cast bronze by combining melted copper with tin, from which they made portraits of their chiefs with a realism seldom surpassed. It is said that the Yorubas taught the Binis how to cast bronze when the royal bronze-smith Ighe-Igha was sent to teach them the art. On the foundations of Yoruba culture, the Binis later built an empire of their own that survived for more than five hundred years.

In 1668, a Dutch explorer named Dapper visited the Bini capital of Benin and recorded his impressions of the town. He wrote that the chief's court was square, divided into many marvelous dwellings with spacious passageways between. The streets were very straight and clean, and many of the houses had roof posts covered with cast copper engravings. He also saw the royal treasury, which was hidden behind a white carpet in the royal chambers of the chief. Included were eleven bronze heads, each wearing a headdress carved from an elephant's tooth, representing the spirits of ancient Bini chiefs.

Dapper also must have seen several identical masks showing the face of a man magnificently carved in ivory. They were designed to be worn on the chief's belt as sacred emblems of his rule. Made in the sixteenth century, they were passed down from old chiefs to their successors for almost four hundred years until 1897. At that time the British army invaded Benin and took the entire royal

Bronze head (British museum cast).
Ife, Yoruba tribe, Nigeria, c. fourteenth century.
(Courtesy of the American Museum of Natural History)

treasury. Thousands of bronze and ivory sculptures were shipped to England, where they astounded scholars by their quality and developed style. No one had expected to see such beautiful art from the "primitive" African world.

Belt mask, court of Benin, Bini tribe, Nigeria, c. 1550.
(Courtesy of the Museum of Primitive Art, New York)

4/   Images of Power

To trace the next development in the history of sculpture, we must go back more than five thousand years to the fertile plains of western Asia and Egypt. There, in the Mesopotamian valley beside the Tigris and Euphrates rivers, and in Egypt along the banks of the Nile, the first city cultures were born. In the beginning, the people of Mesopotamia and Egypt were farmers living in simple villages, much like other people of Africa or New Guinea. But the land they cultivated was so rich that they were able to produce more food than they needed. They started to trade extra grain with neighboring tribes, establishing routes of travel between them. Eventually, their villages merged into single, large communities that were ruled by the most powerful kings.

In their cities, the Mesopotamians and Egyptians created the first organized societies in history. They set up laws that all citizens were expected to obey, and they appointed priests who enforced the rules of religion. They discovered how to cast metals to make improved weapons and tools. They invented systems of writing and arithmetic to keep their accounts in order. They built enormous palaces, temples, and tombs for their kings with the labor of thousands of people and made many sculptures in praise of the kings and gods.

Mesopotamia

Throughout the long history of Mesopotamia, city-states rose and fell, each creating their own monumental buildings and sculptures of their kings. The people of these city-states thought that sculptures made their kings immortal simply because their true likenesses were re-created in permanent form. So strong was this belief that invading armies even cut the head off the enemy king's statue in order to rob him of life after death. A statue of Gudea, governor of Lagash, who reigned about 2150 B.C., when the Sumerians were in power, has survived. An inscription on the statue in Sumerian writing offered thanks to Gudea for building a temple and hoped that his life would be long.

More than a thousand years later, when the Assyrians controlled Mesopotamia, the courage and physical strength of the kings were honored above everything else. In the palace at Nineveh, which was built in the seventh century B.C., long scenes of King Ashurbanipal leading his troops to war were sculpted in relief on the walls. On other walls he was shown in his chariot, aiming his bow and arrow in the midst of a lion hunt. He wore a crown and his beard was elaborately curled. Behind him his servants speared an attacking lion, while five others lay dying in the distance. This

Seated figure of
Gudea, Mesopotamia,
c. 2100 B.C.
(The Metropolitan
Museum of Art,
Harris Brisbane
Dick Fund, 1959)

Winged bull from the palace of Nimrud, Mesopotamia, ninth century B.C.
(The Metropolitan Museum of Art, Gift of John D. Rockefeller, 1932)

scene was made to immortalize Ashurbanipal's bravery and cruelty in the hunt, which were respected almost as much as his military prowess.

The Assyrians also made sculptures of guardian figures, combining human faces with the forms of different animals as symbols of superhuman strength. In Nimrud, at the palace of Ashurnasipal II, who reigned between 883 and 859 B.C., a huge winged bull stood guard at the gate. Its face, with its crown and curly beard, looked like the king, and its wings looked like those of an eagle. Its body was carved with realistic detail, except that it was sculpted to have five legs. In this way, the bull would appear complete from every side, even if one of its legs was temporarily hidden from view. This sculpture was made to suggest that the figure possessed the wisdom of a man, the power of a bull, and the swiftness of an eagle, and that it would stand guard at the gate for eternity through the sculpted form.

Egypt

The Egyptians made sculptures to show the immortality of their kings, not necessarily to describe military power. Theirs was a more stable society, protected from invasion by vast deserts that allowed them a security the Mesopotamians could not enjoy. For nearly three thousand years, the Egyptians were never forced to change, which led them to believe that they could preserve their empire forever.

In many ways, the Egyptians succeeded. Near the pyramids at Gizeh, they carved the Sphinx, a huge stone sculpture that has stood

Sphinx of Gizeh, Egyptian, IV Dynasty. (The Bettmann Archive)

guarding the Nile Valley for more than five thousand years. Buried beneath the sand was the reclining body of a lion, 146 feet long, from which rose the head of a man, almost 29 feet high. Steps were cut into the stone from the head to the space between the lion's paws, where an altar to Harmachis, the god of the morning sun, used to be. A causeway led from the Sphinx to the tomb of the pharaoh Chephren, which was hidden deep inside the second pyramid of Gizeh. The face of the Sphinx is thought to resemble Chephren, who ruled Egypt in the Old Kingdom period, about 2580 B.C.

Inside the tombs, the Egyptians sculpted scenes of daily life so that the dead could spend eternity surrounded by familiar things. They showed people gathering grain or catching birds in the papyrus plants, women brewing beer, or farmers with their plows. In trying to capture reality, they made their sculptures as true to nature as they could, while they followed strict, partly religious rules that governed their artistic style.

According to the strict rules, statues of people had to face the front in stiff, unmoving positions, with their arms held close to their bodies and their left feet ahead of the right. Sculptures in relief had to show people with their heads and legs in profile, but their eyes and shoulders placed as if seen from the front. People were always made bigger than other things because they were considered more important: a man was sculpted larger than a tree or shown too big to pass through the doorway of a house.

For one short period during the reign of the pharaoh Akhenaten,

---

King Sahu-Ré and companion, Egyptian, V Dynasty, Berlin Museum.
(The Metropolitan Museum of Art, Rogers Fund, 1918)

Queen Nefertiti, Egyptian, XVIII Dynasty, Berlin Museum. (The Bettmann Archive)

beginning about 1375 B.C., Egypt was almost freed from its rigid traditions. Akhenaten tried to break the power of the priests to gain absolute rule for himself. He established a new religion, making Aten, the life-giving sun disk, the highest god of all, and even took Aten's name as his own to show how closely they were related. He encouraged artists to sculpt nature as it truly was, to show freely the beauty of Aten's creations.

The sculptors found a worthy subject in Nefertiti, Akhenaten's queen. She is thought to have been a Hittite princess from Mesopotamia, who brought new ideas from her homeland that influenced her husband's reforms. Not only was she influential, she was also very beautiful, as we can see from her portrait carved in limestone. Her face was sculpted naturally, without regard for the old rules that made earlier sculptures so stiff. The details of her makeup and the patterns of her headdress were carefully painted with colors. Unfortunately for the art of Egypt, the climate of freedom that allowed this beautiful portrait to be made was destroyed when Akhenaten died. The old traditions were brought back again to remain for the life of the empire.

Ancient Mexico

For more than a thousand years before the birth of Christ until the arrival of the Spanish in the sixteenth century A.D., civilizations rose in Mexico and Central America which shared many things in common with the empires of Egypt and Mesopotamia. They were city cultures that owed their development to the abundance of food and that discovered many skills and crafts, including astronomy

and writing. They worshiped their kings for their tremendous power and had castes of priests, controlled by the kings, which enforced the laws of religion. They even built pyramids, some of them larger than the pyramids of Gizeh, as bases for temples which stood on the top, reaching toward the heavens.

One of the greatest civilizations of ancient America was that of the Maya, who lived in the Yucatan Peninsula, southern Mexico, and Guatemala. Their culture reached its height between the third and ninth centuries A.D. The Maya seem to have been a peaceful people, more concerned with knowledge and art than with establishing powerful empires. They built many cities as religious centers, with beautifully constructed pyramids and temples decorated with finely made sculptures.

In many of their cities, the Maya carved huge stone altars for the temples, showing the figures of rulers and gods. They sculpted tall stone columns called *stelae*, which were carved in relief with picture symbols, recording their history and measuring the movement of the stars. They made mosaic funerary masks and pendant heads, fitting together pieces of pearl shell, obsidian, and jade. They modeled delicate figures in clay, some to be used as whistles or incense burners, others representing spirits. They also excelled in wood carving, as is shown in this proud figure of a kneeling man. This statue is the only Maya wood sculpture known to have survived.

For unknown reasons, the Maya suddenly stopped recording their history about 790. Within a hundred years, many of their cities were mysteriously abandoned, the temples and sculptures

---

Kneeling Figure, Maya, fifth-sixth century.
(Courtesy of the Museum of Primitive Art, New York)

left to fall into ruins. Perhaps they were affected by the great up-heavals then occurring in the north. Nomadic people, hungry for power, were migrating southward, bringing warlike gods and new ideas.

In the north, nomadic people called the Toltecs moved into central Mexico and, according to ancient chronicles, founded the city of Tula in 856. Their arrival marked the beginning of a long period of conflict and unrest. Through military force, they imposed their will on most of central Mexico until 1168, when their city was destroyed by new nomadic groups, and the Toltecs were forced to flee to the south. Eventually, some of them settled in the old Maya city of Chichén Itzá, where they built temples to their gods and established a new civilization.

One of the most familiar sculptures made by the Toltecs was the figure of Chac-Mool, the god of rain, which they left wherever they settled. The god was usually shown reclining comfortably with his head turned to the side. He wore a headdress quite like that of the Sphinx of Gizeh, and his eyes had the same stark, immovable stare. In his lap he held a bowl, whether for tribute or sacrifice no one is certain. Many of these statues were found in Chichén Itzá, placed by the doorway to the Temple of the Warriors.

The Toltecs' military spirit and belief in warlike gods found their final expression with the Aztecs, the last people of ancient Mexico. Originally, the Aztecs had been an unwanted band of nomads who finally settled down in 1325. In a remarkably short time, they built the city of Tenochtitlán — where Mexico City stands today — into the gleaming capital of a vast and powerful empire.

More than any other people before them, the Aztecs were controlled by their belief in the needs of terrifying gods. They thought that many of their gods required human sacrifices in order to renew

Chac-Mool, Toltec-Maya, Museo Nacional, Mexico City. (Museo Nacional, Mexico)

their strength. The sun god demanded a daily ration of human blood to continue his course through the sky, which kept the common people in mortal fear of being dragged off to the sacrifice. Many people thought that their only purpose in life was to make blood offerings to these gods, whose sculpted images waited hungrily in the temples.

A Spanish soldier named Bernal Díaz reached Tenochtitlán in

1519 and there saw the temples and idols. He described one of the sculptures as being a gigantic stone figure with a wide face and huge, disgusting eyes, its body covered with gold, pearls, and jewels. It wore a necklace of gold faces and silver hearts decorated with brilliant blue stones. Around its feet coiled enormous snakes, also covered with gold and gems, and in its hands it held a bow and arrows. Near the sculpture, priests were burning eight human hearts, and the sanctuary was black with splattered blood. This idol represented Huitzilopochtli, the Aztec god of war, who was also the incarnation of the sun.

The Aztec Empire met its end when the Spanish conquistador Hernando Cortés finally conquered Tenochtitlán in 1521. Thus ended the long and creative history of the ancient Mexican civilizations. The Mesopotamian and Egyptian empires met a similar fate when the Persians conquered them in the sixth century B.C. But their ideas had already spread to the islands and mainland of Greece. There they took root and flowered in an entirely new form that led to the first true representation of man.

5/ Images of Man

The city-states of ancient Greece first came into contact with Egypt and Mesopotamia about 700 B.C., when trading routes were established. Sailors and traders returned from their journeys laden with beautiful carpets, embroidered fabrics, and engraved metal pots and bowls, all richly decorated with imaginary beasts and birds. Greek artists quickly adapted what they saw, working the strange winged animals, griffins, and sphinxes into new designs of their own.

They also learned to make sculptures of the human figure that would stand upright with no support. At first they copied the stiff Egyptian style, making the figures face the front with one foot ahead of the other. But soon their curious minds were not satisfied with such rigid rules, and they began to seek new ways to bring vitality to their sculptures.

One of the Greeks' first discoveries was to make a smile. It seems like a simple thing to make a smile, but when something has never been done before, it takes imagination and courage to do it. They

carved the smile on each *kouros* (figure of a young man) and on each *kore* (figure of a young woman). In fact, they carved the same smile on the faces of most of their sculptures for nearly two hundred years.

In 480 B.C., the city-state of Athens defeated the Persians at the battle of Salamis. Greece's era of greatness began. Revolutionary ideas were free to flourish: the idea of democracy, which held that the laws of a country should be made by citizens voting in public assemblies; the idea that man himself, as Socrates said, was truly the marvel of the world. People were no longer regarded as victims of natural forces or the frightened subjects of kings. They were individuals with intelligent minds, able to reason and to understand.

For the first time in history, sculptors were not nameless craftsmen but respected men free to express their own creative ideas. They were even allowed to sign their works, which gave them new ambition and pride. With great enthusiasm and inquiring minds, they set out to learn how the human body really appeared, how its muscles, curves, and lines all moved together. They combined this knowledge with geometric designs to create figures true to nature, yet more perfect than nature could ever be, just as they believed that man, with his intelligence and wisdom, was the highest creation of the gods.

In the *Discus Thrower* by the sculptor Myron, we can see an example of this ideal. The athlete's weight rests on his right leg as his body and arms swing to the left, creating two directions of motion. The line of his right arm flows down through his shoulders

---

Kore, Greek, sixth century B.C.
(Courtesy of The Press and Information Service of Greece)

into his left arm to create a circle, which is repeated in the line of his back and again in the shape of the disc. Even the angles of space between his body and arms seem the same as the angle at the bend of his legs, creating an impression of perfect balance, with each form in relation to the others.

As the *Discus Thrower* was the ideal of a body in motion, the *Doryphorus,* or Spear Bearer, by the sculptor Polyclitus was the ideal of a body in repose. (See page 45.) The lines of the Spear Bearer's body appear less measured, yet even in the figure's relaxation we sense movement and life, an organization of forms that rhythmically flow together.

In 449 B.C., under the enlightened leadership of Pericles, it was decided to rebuild the Acropolis, a rock citadel in Athens where temples to the gods had stood until the Persians burned them down. Pericles envisioned monuments of such splendor that they would bring everlasting glory to the city, a "beauty in simplicity" that would portray the spirit and ambition of man. He appointed the sculptor Phidias to oversee the work and employed the labor of the Athenian citizens.

The main building on the Acropolis was the Parthenon, temple to the maiden goddess Athena Parthenos, who was also the goddess of truth and wisdom — spirit of the Athenian dream. It was built from large sections of marble, with rows of columns each so delicately curved that no eye could see they were not straight. Above the columns and beneath the roof, beautiful sculptures were carved depicting scenes from Athena's life. All the figures were sculpted with absolute mastery of form, in magnificent design and detail.

Myron: *The Discus Thrower,* Greek, c. 460 B.C. (Roman copy), Museo delle Terme, Rome. (Scala New York/Florence)

Near the Parthenon, a smaller temple called the Erechtheum was built in honor of Erechtheus. This legendary founder of Athens was said to have been born on the Acropolis and raised by Athena herself. Sculptures of women, called *caryatids,* were used instead of columns to support the roof of the porch. Their bodies were thrust slightly forward and their shoulders held back as they gracefully bore the weight. Their supple stance and the soft lines of their robes were much more natural than the rigid beauty of the *kore* with the ancient smile.

But the Athenians were given little time to enjoy their marvelous accomplishments. In 429 B.C., Pericles died of the plague and Phidias had already been disgraced by jealous rivals. In 404 B.C., Athens was conquered by Sparta, a Greek city-state ruled by stern military men. A period of unrest followed. Sculptors reflected the change by turning away from the purity of their earlier ideals to more romantic subjects. The sculptor Praxiteles made statues of beautiful women to represent Aphrodite, the goddess of love, carving the marble so softly that they appear as if in a dream. Later, others even chose subjects like old people, wrinkled and bent with age, as if expressing through cruel reality the less hopeful truth of the times.

In 334 B.C., a new force rose up in Greece that changed the direction of culture once again. Alexander of Macedon, a young military genius, inherited his father's army and set out to conquer the world. He took with him poets, sculptors, and works of art to spread the greatness of Greek ideas. By the time he died at age thirty-three, he had claimed a vast empire that extended through Egypt and Meso-

Polyclitus: *The Spear Bearer,* Greek, c. 450 B.C. (Roman copy), Museo Nazionale, Naples. (Scala New York/Florence)

potamia, across Persia, all the way to India. But his empire did not stay whole for long. After his death, the generals who had served him so loyally carved up his conquests into dynasties of their own and spent their time warring with one another in a constant struggle for power.

During this period, called the Hellenistic Age, sculpture turned back to what it had been in the empires of old. No longer was it an attempt to define the perfect nature of man, but was more concerned with showing the wealth and greatness of kings. Great monuments were erected, like the Colossus of Rhodes, a gigantic bronze statue so large that its fingers alone were the size of a normal person. One of the Seven Wonders of the Ancient World, it was said to have stood astride the harbor at Rhodes so that ships sailed in and out between its enormous legs. In 224 B.C. it was shaken down by an earthquake, and for hundreds of years the huge pieces of bronze lay strewn on the ground exactly where they had fallen.

At the end of the Hellenistic Age, sculpture turned from monumental works to a more emotional expression of form designed to provoke the feelings of the viewer. Groups of people were sculpted together caught up in dramatic events. The *Laocoön,* which was carved by three sculptors from Rhodes about 50 B.C., shows the legendary priest of Troy and his sons being devoured by two water snakes for having offended the god Apollo. Their bodies twist in horror as their limbs are entangled by the writhing snakes, and we can only feel, as the artists intended, their terror of approaching death.

The Laocoön, Greek, first century B.C., Vatican Museum.
(The Bettmann Archive)

Perhaps the drama of *Laocoön* prophesied the fate of Greece, for just as its marble forms were being carved, the powerful armies of Rome were establishing themselves as masters of the Mediterranean world. Greece's age of greatness came to an end, but its ideas were never conquered. They lived on to influence not only the Romans, but centuries of civilization beyond.

Rome

The Romans loved Greek sculpture. They transported many Greek masterpieces to Rome and brought artists from all over Greece to make copies of the original works. Sculptures by Myron, Polyclitus, Phidias, Praxiteles, and others were duplicated and placed in the spacious gardens and villas of the rich. Through these copies, much of Greek sculpture has survived, for most of the original statues were destroyed or lost ages ago.

Before conquering Greece, the Romans had already inherited artistic ideas from the Etruscans, whose culture had dominated the Italian peninsula until the mid-fourth century B.C. The Etruscans had never shared the Greek ideal of the perfect nature of man, but had tried through their art to capture the truth of a person's appearance. The Romans combined this idea with Greek knowledge of the human form to make portrait sculptures that were very realistic in style. They tried to show the personality of an individual through the shape of the face, finding character in a jagged nose, keen eyes, or a rugged jaw. Even senators and wealthy patrons were shown as they appeared, without being made to look more perfect than they actually were.

Bust of an Unknown
Man, Roman, first
century B.C.
(The Metropolitan
Museum of Art,
Rogers Fund, 1912)

After the empire had grown to include most of the then-known world, Roman portrait sculpture lost some of its trueness to life. Powerful rulers seem mainly to see themselves as superior human beings, and in Rome they were no exception. Portraits of the emperors showed them as handsome, brave, or wise — whatever they imagined themselves to be — sometimes combining natural images of their faces with bodies of heroic design. A huge bronze statue of Emperor Trebonianus Gallus, who reigned between A.D. 251 and 253, showed the emperor's face as it probably appeared, with its

wrinkles and puffy cheeks, yet his body was modeled on such a gigantic scale that it seemed possessed of superhuman might.

Despite the vanity of power, Roman portrait sculpture never entirely lost its realistic sense of truth until the very end of the empire. Then, in the early fourth century, the emperor Constantine became the first Roman ruler to embrace the Christian faith. In 330 he moved the capital from Rome to Byzantium, in what is now modern Turkey. There he founded the city of Constantinople, which later became the center of a new empire after Rome fell to barbarian hordes.

A new influence was felt in sculpture. In the portrait of Constantine his eyes are uplifted to heaven as if in prayer, his massive head stiffly placed to the front without motion or living expression. He seems almost godlike in a trance of religious awe. This sculpture marks the beginning of the Christian age, an era of faith that inspired the art of the Western world for the next one thousand years.

Head of Constantine, Roman, fourth century.
(The Metropolitan Museum of Art, Bequest of Mary Clark Thompson, 1926)

6/   The Christian Age

The Christian idea of the world was based on the belief that man could save his soul through faith. By participating in the holy mysteries of the Church and seeking forgiveness for his sins, he could gain God's blessing and ascend into heaven when he died. His thoughts and hopes were turned away from the real world to the spiritual realm of heaven, where God and the Holy Family dwelled in everlasting life.

In Byzantium, a new style of art developed to serve the Christian beliefs. The realism of Greek and Roman art was abandoned because it was concerned with mortal things. Instead, artists tried to create images of spiritual beings who existed beyond the earth. They portrayed Jesus and Mary and a host of angels looming in space, free from all of nature's laws. In one ivory book cover carved in relief, the figure of Mary seems to float as if resting on a cloud. She is made much larger than the other figures so as to point out her spiritual importance. Even the Infant Jesus beside her is shown

Virgin and Child,
Byzantine, eleventh
century. (The
Metropolitan Museum
of Art, Gift
of J. Pierpont
Morgan, 1927)

bigger than the cow and sheep that peek over the edge of his crib.

The Byzantine style was not the least bit suited to sculpture. Sculpture was round; it represented material shapes. The Christian idea called for spiritual illusion. Every effort was made to avoid volume, so that sculptures got flatter and flatter until they almost disappeared. Finally, in the eighth century, Emperor Leo Isauricus banned them altogether for daring to show spiritual beings in actual physical form.

However, in those days most Christians were simple people who could neither read nor write, and it soon became apparent that they needed sculpted images to guide them in the faith. Sculptures were allowed once again, but only if they showed the Holy Family in solemn poses without movement or expressions of life. The ivory statuette (page 53) of the Virgin and Child shows how stiffly the figures were carved. Their forms and the rigid lines of their robes were given practically no volume at all.

Northern Europe and the Romanesque Style

The Byzantine style spread throughout the Mediterranean world and to the northern parts of Europe, where the barbarian tribes of Franks and Goths were just beginning to settle down. In the eighth century, Charlemagne, the king of the Franks, who had traveled to the south and seen the art himself, made a deliberate effort to bring

Statue of Joseph, detail from *The Adoration of the Magi*, Spanish, twelfth century.

(The Metropolitan Museum of Art, Cloisters Collection, 1930)

the styles northward. The people of the north eagerly adopted the new ideas, for their own artistic traditions were limited to the few ornaments and decorated utensils that they had been able to carry in their old nomadic life.

In the north, Christians soon felt a growing need to build large churches in which all could assemble to pray. At first they copied an old Roman building called a *basilica,* a style that had been introduced by Charlemagne. The basilica was a long, rectangular structure originally designed as a covered market. The Christians added a section that cut across the building to give it the shape of the cross.

Then, in the eleventh century in France, a sudden burst of creative energy led to the development of a new type of church, with rounded arches and a vaulted ceiling that allowed the roof to be raised. This style was called Romanesque, named after those parts of Europe that had once been Roman provinces. Inspired Christians, especially in France, England, and Spain, set to work to build the new churches — with marvelous results for sculpture.

Suddenly there were thousands of new corners, arches, doorways, and pillars that cried out for sculptural forms. Romanesque artists did not limit themselves to the rigid Byzantine style, but drew freely from every possible source. They took designs from their own pagan past, animals from ancient Mesopotamia, fragments from Rome, and scenes from the Scriptures and molded them into a vigorous style of their own. They invented fantastic monsters whose weird forms were squeezed into crowded niches, some with human heads, lions' bodies, and scorpions' tails. Once again figures were sculpted without fear of showing expression or life, like the statue of Joseph shown in a most human pose — resting his head in his hand as he sleeps (page 55).

The Gothic Style

About 1125 in the Ile-de-France, the region around the city of Paris, the Gothic cathedral evolved. Brilliant architects discovered how to expand the rounded arches of Romanesque churches into pointed arches, and to brace the walls with arched supports. These discoveries allowed soaring vaults to be built, which made the whole structure rise weightlessly into the sky. Even the stones themselves seemed to triumph over matter, making the Gothic cathedral a perfect expression of the most spiritual Christian beliefs.

New areas became available for sculptures. The cramped positions afforded by Romanesque churches were replaced by tall, vertical spaces that allowed room for more natural figures. At Strasbourg Cathedral, this statue of the Virgin once stood, offering her quiet blessing. She is shown with a solemn and holy dignity, yet her face and figure are much closer to life than statues in the Romanesque style.

The new interest in naturalism was encouraged by the teachings of Francis of Assisi, which came to be known at this time. Francis believed in the joy of the natural world. He preached to the birds, regarding them as his brothers, and wrote religious songs to the sun. He inspired artists to turn to nature for their models, to find beauty in lifelike forms. An example of his influence can be seen in a Gothic sculpture made in the fourteenth century, which shows the Virgin Mary when she learned she was to be the mother of God. Her gracious beauty and the ease of her pose show how natural sculpture had become.

Virgin from the Cathedral of Strasbourg, French, mid-thirteenth century. (The Metropolitan Museum of Art, Cloisters Collection, 1947)

Virgin of the Annunciation, French, fourteenth century. (The Metropolitan Museum of Art, Gift of J. Pierpont Morgan, 1917)

7 /   The Renaissance

Although the Gothic style spread throughout most of Europe, it never really penetrated into Italy. There, in the thirteenth century, a sculptor named Nicola Pisano, his son Giovanni, and his pupil Andrea began a course of development that led Italy in a distinct direction of its own. They turned away from the religious style of the north to study the ruins of Roman art and architecture and tried to revive the ancients' belief in the great nobility of man.

In the fourteenth century, a temporary Gothic influence held up the revival of ancient ideas. But in the fifteenth century the Gothic style was driven out altogether, and Italy was free to direct all of its creative might to the glory of the pre-Christian past. This period was called the Renaissance, which means "rebirth," and a rebirth it truly was. For the first time in more than one thousand years, man became the center of his own beliefs. What his reason and intelligence could not understand was rejected as being unworthy of his greatness. He became the "measure of all things," the thinking being who alone had the ability to give order and beauty to the world.

During this time, artists were no longer regarded as mere craftsmen in the service of the Church, but were elevated to positions of respect for the brilliant gifts they possessed. Rich and powerful princes and popes vied with one another for their time, commissioning works in the belief that art was man's greatest achievement. Each artist developed a style of his own, drawing freely from the accomplishments of other artists and from the lessons of the ancient past.

One of the first artists after Pisano to study seriously the ruins of ancient Rome was Lorenzo Ghiberti (1378–1455). According to Giorgio Vasari, a painter who wrote a book about Renaissance artists in 1550, Ghiberti was the son of a goldsmith who learned his father's art and went on to become the greatest bronze-caster in the fifteenth century. Ghiberti's masterpieces were the bronze doors for the Baptistery in the city of Florence, which took him almost his whole life to complete. The doors were divided into many panels modeled in relief, each showing a different scene from the Old Testament. Ghiberti made the reliefs on various levels so that some figures stood out with definite form while others seemed barely raised, creating an illusion of depth and space.

In the panel showing the Creation of Adam and Eve, we can see Adam in the lower left corner being raised up from the earth by God. Eve stands on the right side, already filled with life. Their figures are modeled with almost as much volume as freestanding sculptures. The figures in the middle part of the scene are less rounded, so that they appear farther away, while the figures beneath the trees and the angels on top are given practically no volume at

Lorenzo Ghiberti: *The Creation of Adam and Eve,* east door, Baptistery, Florence, 1425–52. (The Bettmann Archive)

Jacopo della Quercia: *The Creation,*
main door, Church of San Petronio, Bologna, 1425–35. (Alinari/Scala)

all. Ghiberti's sculptures were so delicate and harmonious that a later sculptor named Michelangelo Buonarroti called the doors worthy to be the Gates of Paradise.

Another fifteenth-century sculptor named Jacopo della Quercia (c. 1374–1438) developed a different style that concentrated on showing expression through the human form. He eliminated the delicate modeling of background scenes that Ghiberti had so beautifully created and made bold and simple figures filled with vigorous life. In a panel on the main door of the Church of San Petronio in Bologna, he carved a stone relief depicting his own vision of the Creation. Adam is shown lifting his heavy body as if drawn by an invisible force, expressing through his upheld hand and face his awe of the power of God. The massive figures fill the panel with their energy and are modeled with little detail, a style also deeply admired by Michelangelo Buonarroti.

The most influential sculptor of the fifteenth century in Italy was Donatello (1386–1466). As a young man, Donatello was a student of Ghiberti's, and like him, studied the ruins of ancient Rome. He went on to become a master of both marble and bronze. Through his own powerful ideas, he managed to re-create the art of sculpture in the round by giving dramatic volume and expression to the human form.

His bronze sculpture of the military commander Gattamelata astride a magnificent horse showed the influence of ancient Roman art. The commander's figure was heroic in its self-confident pose, like the statues of ancient Roman emperors. His tired yet defiant

Donatello: Statue of Mary Magdalen (detail), Baptistery, Florence, fifteenth century.
(Courtesy of the Italian Cultural Institute, New York)

face was modeled with the same realism as early Roman portraits, expressing through its weary pride man's hopeless yearning for glory.

Donatello even used ugly forms to create a dramatic effect. In his wooden sculpture of Mary Magdalen (page 65), we see the suffering woman wasted away from lack of food and shelter as she seeks forgiveness for her sins. Her dress is in rags and her tangled hair frames her pitiful face. The modeling of her bony neck and limbs shows how well Donatello understood the human body, whether at the height of its strength like Gattamelata or near death from abuse and starvation. Through ugliness, he created a certain kind of beauty in this statue — a beauty of truth that describes the horror of human despair.

Michelangelo

From the influence of Donatello sprang the most revered sculptor in the history of European art — Michelangelo Buonarroti. Michelangelo was born in a small town near Florence in 1475. When he was thirteen years old, he had already shown such promise at drawing that he was sent to study with the painter Ghirlandaio. When he was fifteen, he was invited to the palace of the powerful Medici family, where he studied sculpture with a man named Bertoldo, who had been a pupil of Donatello's.

One of his early sculptures, completed in 1499, is the *Piéta,* a sculpture of Mary grieving over the body of her son after the Crucifixion. Like Donatello, Michelangelo used his enormous understanding of the human figure to create a masterpiece of form graced by passionate expression. Every detail of the figures — muscles, veins, joints, and folds of the skin and robes — was so perfectly carved that it led Vasari to write: "It is a marvel that the hand of an artist in so short a time can transform shapeless stone into a perfection of beauty seldom achieved by nature."

Soon Michelangelo's extraordinary genius was recognized by all those who loved the beauty of art. In 1505 he was invited to work in Rome by Pope Julius, who commissioned him to design his tomb. While he was there, the ancient Greek statue of the *Laocoön,* which must have been transported from Greece to Rome during the Roman Empire, was discovered buried in a vineyard near the Church of Santa Maria Maggiore. Michelangelo was present when the statue was uncovered and was greatly impressed by the dynamic strength of the figures.

Afterward, perhaps influenced by the heroic *Laocoön,* Michelangelo made sculptures of the human figure with a newfound feeling and power. Two examples can be seen on page 68 in the figures of Night and Day, carved between 1521 and 1525, which recline on the tomb of Giuliano de' Medici in the Church of San Lorenzo in Florence. The feminine but almost manlike figure of Night rests heavily, her head in her hand, while Day, with his rippling muscles, keeps vigil over the tomb. Parts of Day were left unfinished, which creates a variety of texture and heightens the sense of the figure struggling to life from the stone.

In his later years, Michelangelo seldom completed a sculpture, so restless was he in his search for perfect form. His last work, carved between 1555 and 1564 and called the *Rondanini Pietà,* shows Mary holding the body of her son after He has been taken down from the cross. Only Christ's legs were smoothly carved, the rest left in roughly cut planes. Yet, Michelangelo's idea is complete and

Michelangelo: Figures of *Night* (above), and *Day* (below), tomb of Giuliano de' Medici, Basilica of San Lorenzo, Florence, 1521-25. (Courtesy of the New York Public Library)

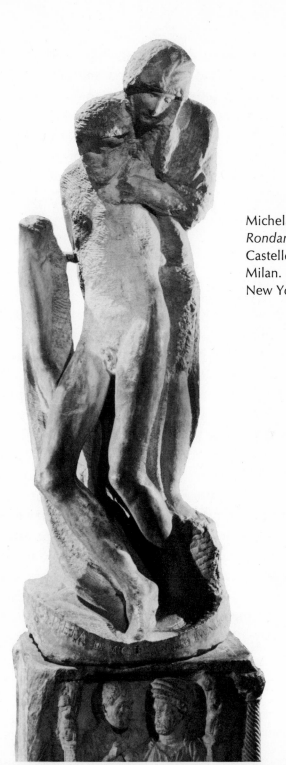

Michelangelo:
Rondanini Pietà,
Castello Sforzesco,
Milan. (Scala
New York/Florence)

is perhaps more dramatically expressed than it would have been if the figures had been carved and polished. Through the simple shapes he devoutly described the mood and weight of their sorrow.

The driving energy that moved Michelangelo to create such beautiful sculptures is best defined in words he spoke himself: "Nothing makes the soul so religious and pure as the endeavor to create something perfect, for God is perfection and whoever strives after perfection is striving for something divine."

The Baroque Style

The achievements of Michelangelo dominated the world of sculpture long after his death in 1564. Later sculptors imitated his style, trying to match his heroic sense of man with exaggerated dramatic forms. Because they lacked his sublime sense of beauty, their works became more and more ornate, seeking through movement, light, and shadow to convey pure emotional feeling. The search for perfection that had guided the master of the Renaissance became of secondary importance.

In the beginning of the seventeenth century, the Catholic church became the strongest force in Italy. Great efforts were needed to fight back the Protestant revolt taking place in northern Europe, so the church used sculpture to direct the attention of the faithful to the glory of God. The resulting style was called baroque, which sought to overwhelm the eyes and emotions of the viewer with passionate religious scenes. Working to please the church, artists lost much of their individuality, as they had in the Christian age.

The height of the baroque style can best be seen in the sculptures

Gian Lorenzo Bernini: *The Ecstasy of Saint Theresa*, Santa Maria della Vittoria, Rome. (The Bettmann Archive)

of Gian Lorenzo Bernini (1598–1680). He was the son of an early baroque sculptor named Pietro, from whom he learned his craft. When Bernini was only nineteen years old, his skill caught the attention of a powerful cardinal, who brought him into the service of the church, where he worked for most of his life.

Like Michelangelo, Bernini was greatly inspired by the ancient statue of the *Laocoön,* whose theatrical pose and rippling marble forms were qualities he admired above all. In Bernini's sculpture called *The Ecstasy of Saint Theresa* (page 71), an altarpiece for the Church of Santa Maria della Vittoria in Rome, the figure of the saint is shown caught in a moment of religious fervor as an angel hovers nearby. Her senses seem overpowered, not by forces such as the water snakes that entwine the *Laocoön,* but by the rapture of her experience with God. The flowing curves of her robe bring the marble to life, inviting the viewer to share in her trance.

The Rococo Style

The emotional style of baroque sculpture spread from Italy to the northern countries, as had the ideas of the Renaissance before. Bernini himself was summoned to France to make portraits of King Louis XIV, who led a magnificent court. There sculptures were made to please the royalty, and although they kept to the baroque style, they were more concerned with showing the elegance of court life than with serving the Catholic church.

In the eighteenth century, French artists developed a style called rococo, based on the baroque but more charming and lighter in spirit. In keeping with the frivolous taste of the court, it avoided a

Jean Antoine Houdon:
Bust of Voltaire, 1781.
(The Metropolitan Museum
of Art, Gift of
J. Pierpont Morgan, 1908)

grandiose vision of man, showing instead his witty and amusing character.

In the portrait of the French writer and philosopher Voltaire, sculpted by Jean Antoine Houdon (1741–1828) in 1781, there is humor in the philosopher's expression. He seems deeply amused yet a bit perplexed at the travails of human experience. This style of sculpture survived until the French Revolution ended the reign of Louis XVI in the last years of the century. Sculptors then turned away from everything that reminded them of the decadent court to look for a purer ideal.

8/   Images of Our Time

In the nineteenth century, after two hundred years of the busy baroque and rococo styles, sculptors turned back once again to the art of ancient Greece. They were not, however, particularly inspired by the ideas that had produced Greek art, as sculptors in the Renaissance had been, but were content merely to imitate its style. As a result, their statues of Greek heroes and gods looked stiff and artificial, and because they were unmoved by a true belief, they had no character or life in their forms. This lack of originality prevailed for most of the century, until, finally, a sculptor appeared who was strong enough to break the chains of the past.

In 1877 in Paris, a French sculptor named Auguste Rodin (1840–1917) exhibited a statue called *The Age of Bronze,* or *Man Awakening to Nature.* It showed the relaxed and natural figure of a youth standing after a heavy sleep. The statue caused a sensation, because in comparison to the other sculptures of the day, it was shockingly realistic in style. Rodin was even accused of making

Auguste Rodin:
The Age of Bronze, 1877.
(The Metropolitan Museum
of Art, Gift of
Mrs. John W. Simpson,
1907)

Auguste Rodin:
Balzac, 1898.
(Philadelphia Museum of Art)

a mold from the body of a living person in order to achieve such a lifelike form. Yet, in spite of the opinions of others, Rodin brought vitality back to sculpture through his honesty and bold ideas.

Rodin was greatly inspired by the sculptures of Michelangelo, with whom he shared the same passionate interest in the human figure. Like Michelangelo, he often left parts of his sculptures unfinished so that the figures seem to struggle to life. In his statue of the French writer Balzac, completed in 1898, he wrapped the body in a roughly cut gown to reveal only its massive weight, and modeled the face in lumpy shapes to show emotion instead of definite features. In this statue, Rodin made more than a portrait. By expressing his own feelings, he infused it with a mysterious grandeur that makes it an image of all mankind.

The Modern Age

The sculptures of Rodin bring us to the twentieth century, an age of science and industry, violence and change. It is a century that has led to a questioning of all previous values, of our beliefs and ways of looking at the world, of our ideas of life itself. Constantly new definitions are placed before us. Endless scientific discoveries produce new shapes for our eyes to see. In order to record the times and give meaningful shape to man's experience, sculpture had to go through a very fundamental change.

Rodin brought new life to sculpture in the beginning of the century. Painters working in Paris brought new ideas. The Spaniard Pablo Picasso (1881–) and the Frenchman Georges Braque (1882–1963) developed a style called cubism, which departed from all European traditions of the past. Finding their inspiration in the bold forms of African tribal sculptures, as well as the work of Post-impressionist painter Paul Cézanne (1839–1906), they tried to reduce the appearance of objects to clear-cut geometrical shapes. They arranged the shapes in logical order with little concern for how the object really looked. The name "cubism" comes from the word "cube" — a measured geometrical form.

Perhaps this difficult idea will become clear if we look at four bronze reliefs sculpted by another French artist, Henri Matisse, (1869–1954). In the first relief, we can see the back view of a woman with her head resting on her arm. The lines of her body are heavy and somewhat distorted, yet we can easily recognize her form. In the second relief, we see the same figure, although this time the artist has simplified the shapes of the woman's body so that the strongest features stand out. In the third relief, he has broken down the forms even more, leaving out practically everything but the line down her back and the heavy weight of her limbs. By the last relief, Matisse has reduced the entire figure to bold geometric volumes that somehow, in spite of their simplicity, still remind us of the original form.

The ideas of cubism were developed even further by other sculptors, including Jacques Lipchitz (1891–). In his work called *Seated Bather,* made in 1917, it is difficult to find any trace of the human figure. Instead, he created a sequence of solid, geometric shapes moving into one another in a purely logical order. Lipchitz did not intend to reproduce an image of a seated person. By analyzing the figure, he wanted to reconstruct it in a rational way, according to his own idea.

Cubism taught a vital lesson to modern sculptors. Suddenly they were free to break down images and rearrange them as they chose or to invent new shapes that had never been made before. It brought them to nonobjective styles. They could explore their private feelings, invent their own beliefs, and create a visual language suited to their world.

One of the masters of our time was Constantin Brancusi, a Romanian sculptor (1876–1957). Brancusi once said that it was impossible to describe the true nature of an object by imitating its

Henri Matisse: *The Back, I, II, III, IV*, 1909–30. (Collection, The Museum of Modern Art, New York, Mrs. Simon Guggenheim Fund)

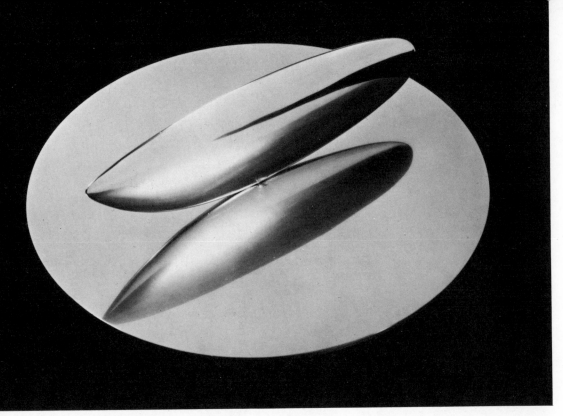

Constantin Brancusi: *The Fish, 1924.* (Courtesy, Museum of Fine Arts, Boston)

outer surface. Reality lay behind the surface in the feeling or movement of the form. In his sculpture called *The Fish,* he made a slender, slippery-looking shape that stands balanced on its finest edge. It seems about to dart away as if suspended for an instant in water. Even though it has no scales, fins, or tail, its pure lines capture the essence of the living creature.

Another important sculptor of the twentieth century is Englishman Henry Moore (1898–). Moore has been inspired both by modern ideas and the sculptures of ancient Mexico, which he admires for the strength of their stony forms. In his *Reclining Woman* we can clearly see a resemblance to the Toltec-Mayan statue of Chac-Mool. The body rests in the same basic position, although in Moore's sculpture the forms are rounder and have more movement.

In a later sculpture called *Reclining Figure, II,* Moore repeated the same basic position, but showed the figure in a less realistic way. This time, he broke the sculpture into two separate parts. On the left, we can see a shape that suggests both the neck and head, the slope of the shoulders, and a heavy arm supporting their weight. On the right, the angular lines of the sculpture suggest blocky legs with knees held in an upright position. This sculpture is like some

Henry Moore: *Reclining Woman,* 1930. (The National Gallery of Canada, Ottawa)

Henry Moore: *Reclining Figure, II,* 1960. (Collection, The Museum of Modern Art, New York. Given in memory of G. David Thompson, Jr., by his father)

frightening but beautiful monster daring us to disturb its timeless pose.

A sculptor with a less heroic vision of the human figure was Swiss-born Alberto Giacometti (1901–66). His small bronze figures are modeled down until they seem wasted away like survivors from a devastating war. They stand or walk in lonely silence, isolated from the rest of mankind. Giacometti said that it was not the outward form of human beings that interested him, but the effect that they had on his inner life.

Alberto Giacometti: *Three Men Walking*, I, 1948–49. (Sidney and Harriet Janis Collection, Gift to the Museum of Modern Art, New York)

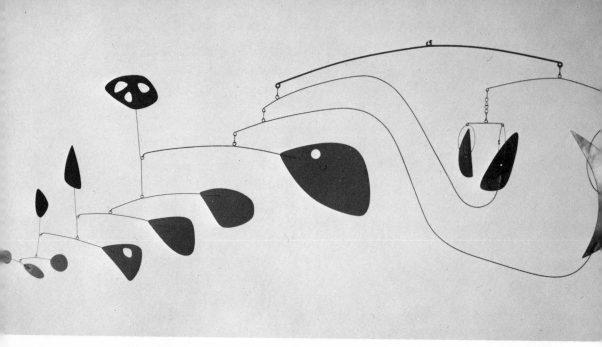

Alexander Calder: *Three Gongs and Red,* c. 1953. (Perls Galleries, New York)

Anthony Caro: *Shadow, 1970.* (Photograph by Andre Emmerich)

Many artists in the twentieth century have turned away from all natural images to explore the ideas and materials of the scientific age. In 1943 an artist named Naum Gabo, who was born in Russia in 1890, made a sculpture called *Linear Construction Number 1*. On a rectangular plastic frame he strung thin plastic threads in a careful design to make a transparent sculpture that seems to have no mass at all. Light penetrates through the form and shimmers on the threads, the way sun touches a spider's web.

The American Alexander Calder (1898–) and the Englishman Anthony Caro (1924–), both trained as engineers, make their sculptures out of steel. By cutting simple shapes out of sheet metal and hanging them on wires, Calder creates structures called *mobiles*, many of which move about if suspended from the ceiling. The forms constantly change their positions and relation to one another if there is the slightest breeze in the room.

Caro welds together large pieces of steel construction beams to make energetic yet balanced designs. The planes of his sculptures move into space like disassembled bridges or buildings that have violently come to life. His works have no reference to any living thing, yet they create in their cold steel forms familiar images of our industrial times.

What are the beliefs of the twentieth century? What guides the hands of sculptors when they try to describe the forces of our world? Do they believe in nature as tribal people did or in blood-thirsty gods or kings? Do they have faith in man as did the ancient Greeks, or in the science that rules our age? These are questions that each sculptor must answer, for each has the freedom to choose. Perhaps, by giving shape to their own beliefs, they can help us to understand ourselves.

A Selected Bibliography

Avery, Catherine, ed. *Classical Handbook*. New York: Appleton, Century Crofts, 1962.

Bazin, Germain. *A History of Art*. New York: Bonanza Books, 1959.

Bowness, Alan. *Modern Sculpture*. New York: Studio Vista, Dutton Picture-back, 1969.

Burroughs, Betty, ed. *Vasari's Lives of the Artists*. New York: Simon and Schuster, 1962.

Disselhoff, H.D. and S. Linné. *Art of Ancient America*. New York: Crown, 1961.

Fagg, William. *African Tribal Images*. Cleveland: Cleveland Museum of Art, The Catherine White Reswick Collection, 1964.

_____. *The Art of Western Africa*. United Nations: Mentor-Unesco Art Book, 1967.

_____. *Nigerian Images*. New York: Praeger, 1963.

Gaunt, William. *The Observer's Book of Sculpture*. New York: Frederick Warne, 1966.

Goldscheider, Ludwig. *Michelangelo*. London: Phaidon Press, 1964.

Metropolitan Museum of Art Guides to the Collections:

    Ancient Near Eastern Art, 1966

Egyptian Art, 1965

Greek and Roman Art, 1964

Medieval Art, 1962

Molesworth, H.D. *European Sculpture*. New York: Praeger, 1965.

Monti, Franco. *African Masks*. London: Paul Hamlyn, 1969.

Murray, Peter and Linda. *The Art of the Renaissance*. New York: Praeger, 1963.

Museum of Primitive Art. *Art of Oceania, Africa and America*. New York.

————. *The Asmat* — The Journal of Michael Clark Rockefeller. New York, 1967.

————. *Sculpture from Africa*. New York, 1963.

Paine, Roberta M. *Looking at Sculpture*. New York: Lothrup, 1968.

Richter, Gisela. *A Handbook of Greek Art*. New York: Phaidon, 1959.

Ritzenthaler, Robert E. *Totem Poles*. Milwaukee Public Museum, 1969.

Rorimer, James J. *The Cloisters*. New York, 1963.

Ruskin, Adriane and Michael Batterberry. *Greek and Roman Art*. New York: McGraw Hill, 1968.

Trowell, Margaret. *Classical African Sculpture*. New York: Praeger, 1964.

Wherry, Joseph. *Indian Masks and Myths*. New York: Funk and Wagnalls, 1969.

Willet, Frank. *Ife in the History of West African Sculpture*. New York: McGraw Hill, 1967.

Index

Numbers in italics indicate illustrations.

About the Author

Penelope Naylor is a painter, illustrator, and writer. She studied sculpture and drawing at Smith College and later in Spain. A professional artist since 1962, she has lived in foreign countries for a number of years — in Spain, Norway, Greece, Mexico, British Columbia, South Africa, Swaziland, and Tanzania. During that time she had many group shows in Europe, Africa, and the United States. In 1964 she painted a large mural for the government of Swaziland, and two years later began to illustrate children's books. Also in 1966 she had a one-man show in New York City, where she now lives with her husband. *Sculpture, The Shapes of Belief* is the author's first book for children.